Dolley Madison
HOSTESS AND PATRIOT

Published by The Child's World®
1980 Lookout Drive • Mankato, MN 56003-1705
800-599-READ • www.childsworld.com

Photographs ©: NorthWind Picture Archives/AP Images, cover, 1; Gilbert Stuart/
AP Images, 5; George Washington Bicentennial Commission/National Archives and
Records Administration, 6; Fotosearch/Archive Photos/Getty Images, 10; Architect of
the Capitol, 13; iStockphoto, 14, 17; Gerry Embleton/NorthWind Picture Archives, 18

ISBN 9781503823969
LCCN 2017944737

Printed in the United States of America
PA02362

ABOUT THE AUTHOR

Emily Rose Oachs graduated as a member of Phi Beta Kappa from the
University of Minnesota with a degree in communication studies. She has
authored more than 50 nonfiction books for children and young adults on
topics ranging from natural disasters and biomes to geography and history.
She lives and writes in Los Angeles.

TABLE OF
CONTENTS

FAST FACTS

Full Name

- Dolley Payne Todd Madison

Birthdate

- May 20, 1768, in Guilford County, North Carolina

Husband

- President James Madison

Children

- John Payne Todd and William Todd

Years in White House

- 1809–1817

Accomplishments

- Saved a portrait of George Washington from the White House in 1814 when British troops invaded during the War of 1812.
- Started the long-standing tradition of First Ladies redecorating the presidential mansion.

- Held Wednesday night gatherings at the White House that helped bring together politicians and gave Dolley an unofficial roll in politics.

Chapter 1

THE PRESIDENTESS

Four hundred people surrounded Dolley Madison and her husband, President James Madison, on the night of his **inauguration**. It was March 4, 1809. They were at the first-ever inaugural ball in Washington, DC. All around, people strained to catch a glimpse of the new president's wife. They called her the "Presidentess."

Even in the sea of guests, Dolley was easy to spot. Her elegant gown of beige velvet had a long train trailing behind. She wore a matching turban of velvet and satin, trimmed with bird-of-paradise feathers.

This stately evening was far different from Dolley's upbringing as a **Quaker**. Dolley Payne was born in a log cabin in Guilford County, North Carolina, in 1768.

◀ Dolley Madison was described as a "national institution."

She grew up on a struggling **plantation** in Virginia. In 1783, Dolley's parents freed the people they had enslaved. Then they moved Dolley and her seven siblings to Philadelphia.

In Philadelphia, Dolley married a Quaker lawyer named John Todd in 1790. Together they had two children. But John and their infant son got sick with yellow fever. They died in 1793.

In 1794, Dolley married James Madison. James was a wealthy slave-owning politician from Virginia. He had helped to draft the young nation's Constitution and Bill of Rights.

James's longtime friend Thomas Jefferson became president in 1801. President Jefferson named James as his secretary of state. Soon after, Dolley and James left Montpelier, their estate in Virginia, for Washington, DC.

While there, Dolley was active in Washington society. Her **gregarious** and generous nature made her well-liked in Washington's social circles. Over time, Dolley became James's political partner. They often discussed political business together. James valued Dolley's opinions. When they were apart, James would send her letters and newspaper articles about current events.

In December 1808, James was elected the fourth president of the United States. Many people believed that Dolley's popularity helped James win the election. Charles C. Pinckney, one of James's challengers for the presidency, remarked, "I was beaten by Mr. and Mrs. Madison. I might have had a better chance had I faced Mr. Madison alone."[2]

Chapter 2

REDECORATING THE WHITE HOUSE

Dolley sat down at her desk with a blank piece of paper in September 1809. She lifted her pen. In even script, she wrote, "Mr. Latrobe." She went on to respond to a letter from the architect Benjamin Henry Latrobe. In it, she discussed their ongoing task of redecorating the White House.

For months, letters between Dolley and Benjamin had shared their ideas for the redecoration. They wanted to turn the White House into a simple, yet elegant space. The pair **scoured** shops all around the East Coast. They shopped in Washington, DC, and Philadelphia, Pennsylvania, for American-made furnishings.

◄ The roles that Dolley took on as First Lady set a precedent for all First Ladies to come.

They also looked in New York, New York, and Baltimore, Maryland. The pair purchased new furniture, curtains, china, silver, and even a piano and guitar.

During this time, a home's appearance was an important symbol of power. Traditionally, men took charge of decorating to control their image. But James trusted Dolley's judgment. He knew he could trust her to help craft his political image. So he had Dolley take over the redecoration of their new home.

Dolley's redecorating set a standard for future First Ladies. Placing her own unique touch on the White House became an unofficial duty of the First Lady.

Benjamin Henry Latrobe also built part of the U.S. Capitol in ▶ Washington, DC.

Chapter 3

MRS. MADISON'S WEDNESDAY NIGHTS

One night in January 1811, the White House was packed with people. Dolley was hosting one of her weekly "drawing rooms," or social gatherings. The lively sound of musicians greeted guests.

Dressed in a satin robe and white turban, Dolley moved freely among her guests. Politicians, writers, young and old, and people of all backgrounds enjoyed the party's music and refreshments. Dolley's charm and kindness were on full display as she stopped to chat with her guests.

Dolley's Wednesday night gatherings began shortly after James's inauguration. No invitation was necessary.

◀ Hundreds of people gathered at the White House to attend Dolley's social gatherings.

The parties quickly became the center of Washington's social life. Dolley arranged for refreshments, such as coffee and ice cream, to be served. Sometimes more than 300 people attended the parties, earning them the nickname "squeezes."

Dolley's Wednesday night gatherings were more than **frivolous** parties. As a woman at that time, Dolley was unable to take an official role in politics. Yet these parties gave her the chance to informally participate.

Dolley also used these gatherings as a way to "destroy **rancorous** feeling" between political opponents, according to Dolley's sister.[3] Holding parties in the drawing rooms allowed Dolley to build bridges between politicians.

"In a few minutes I emerged from the dirt and darkness into the blazing splendor of Mrs. Madison's drawing-room."[4]

— *Washington Irving, writer and historian*

▲ The East Room is the largest room in the White House and has been used for holding many events, including dances and press conferences.

Because of the connections she made, Dolley was able to win support for James on many topics. It was a position the First Lady had never taken before.

Chapter 4

SAVING GENERAL WASHINGTON

Dolley Madison climbed to the roof of the White House on August 24, 1814. She "turn[ed] her spy glass in every direction," she later wrote her sister.[5] She was scanning the horizon for American soldiers and her husband. In the distance, she heard the boom of cannon fire.

The United States was in the midst of the War of 1812. British troops were moving toward the nation's capital. Most of Washington, DC's population had already fled the city. Yet Dolley remained. "I am determined not to go myself until I see Mr. Madison is safe," she said.[6]

◀ Dolley not only saved the portrait of George Washington in 1814, but she also saved the Declaration of Independence.

Finally, Dolley had no choice but to leave. She had already filled her carriage with important government documents. Before she left, Dolley stopped at a large portrait of George Washington. "Save that picture!" she cried.[7]

Dolley knew she could not leave without saving the portrait. It was an important symbol for the young nation. If the British found it, they would mock and destroy it.

The portrait's frame was screwed to the wall. Dolley instructed an enslaved servant named Paul Jennings to break the frame. Then they rolled up the canvas and gave the portrait to friends to keep safe. Dolley fled.

Just hours later, the British reached Washington, DC. They **looted** the White House and lit it on fire. The White House burned down. It had to be rebuilt in 1817. Had Dolley not rescued the portrait, her fears might have come true. Rescuing Washington's portrait may be the act that Dolley is best known for today.

Dolley Madison remained beloved by the American people for the rest of her life. When she died in 1849, hundreds attended her funeral, including President Zachary Taylor and many members of Congress. It was the largest funeral Washington, DC, had ever hosted. Its immense size showed that even years after her husband had left office, Dolley's **influence** lived on.

THINK ABOUT IT

- Women of her time were not allowed to participate in politics, but many of Dolley's actions as First Lady were political. How did her actions support her country and her husband's presidency?
- What traits help make a political figure become beloved by the public? How do you think Dolley's traits accomplished that?
- Why do you think Americans so greatly admired Dolley for saving George Washington's portrait? What did this action symbolize to the American people?

GLOSSARY

frivolous (FRIH-voh-lus): Frivolous describes something that is not important or serious. Parties may be seen as frivolous and without any important purpose.

gregarious (greh-GAYR-ee-us): Gregarious describes a person who is social and enjoys the company of others. Gregarious Dolley Madison enjoyed hosting her weekly White House parties.

inauguration (in-awg-yur-AY-shun): An inauguration is a ceremony in which a person is sworn into office. James Madison's inauguration marked the beginning of his presidency.

influence (IN-flew-ehns): An influence is the power or effect of something or someone. Dolley had great influence over Washington, DC, throughout her life.

looted (LOOT-ed): A place has been looted when things have been stolen from it during war. British soldiers stole food and clothing when they looted the White House.

plantation (plan-TAY-shun): A plantation is a large farm. As a child, Dolley's parents grew crops on their plantation.

propriety (proh-PRY-i-tee): To behave with propriety means to be proper and have good manners. People said Dolley acted with great propriety during her Wednesday night gatherings.

Quaker (KWAY-ker): A Quaker is a member of the Christian religious group known as the Society of Friends. Dolley grew up as a Quaker.

rancorous (RAN-kor-us): Rancorous describes something that is filled with intense hatred or ill will. Opposing politicians sometimes had rancorous arguments.

SOURCE NOTES

1. "Dolley Payne Todd Madison." *Whitehouse.gov.* USA.gov, n.d. Web. 19 June 2017.

2. Catherine Allgor. *A Perfect Union: Dolley Madison and the Creation of the American Nation.* New York: Henry Holt and Company, 2006. Print.

3. Ibid.

4. Allen C. Clark. *Life and Letters of Dolley Madison.* Washington, DC: Press of W.F. Roberts Company, 1914. Print.

5. David B. Mattern and Holly C. Shulman, eds. *The Selected Letters of Dolley Payne Madison.* Charlottesville: University of Virginia Press, 2003. Print.

6. Thomas Fleming. "When Dolley Madison Took Command of the White House." *Smithsonian Magazine,* March 2010. Web. 4 Apr. 2017.

7. Catherine Allgor. *A Perfect Union: Dolley Madison and the Creation of the American Nation.* New York: Henry Holt and Company, 2006. Print.

TO LEARN MORE

Books

Kent, Zachary. *Dolley Madison: "The Enemy Cannot Frighten a Free People."* Berkeley Heights, NJ: Enslow Publishers, 2010.

Krull, Kathleen. *Women Who Broke the Rules: Dolley Madison.* New York, NY: Bloomsbury, 2015.

Pastan, Amy. *First Ladies.* New York, NY: DK Publishing, 2017.

Web Sites

Visit our Web site for links about Dolley Madison:

childsworld.com/links

Note to Parents, Teachers, and Librarians: We routinely verify our Web links to make sure they are safe and active sites. So encourage your readers to check them out

INDEX